Hull, Mary
The horse in harness

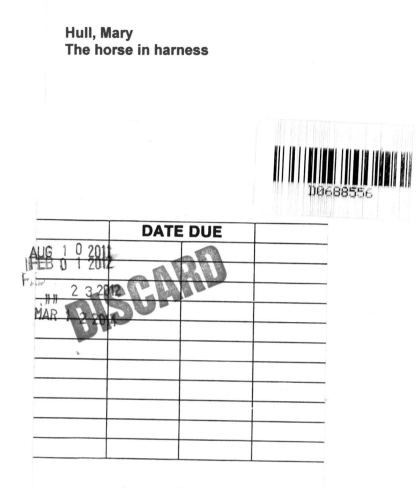

DATE DUE			
AUG 1 0 2011			
FEB 0 1 2012			
FEB 2 3 2012			
MAR 1 2 2014			

THE HORSE LIBRARY

THE HORSE LIBRARY

THE HORSE
IN HARNESS

MARY E. HULL

CHELSEA HOUSE PUBLISHERS

PHILADELPHIA

Frontis: Deb Ladaroute guides her horse through a water obstacle during the cross-country competition at a combined driving event.

CHELSEA HOUSE PUBLISHERS

EDITOR IN CHIEF Sally Cheney
ASSOCIATE EDITOR IN CHIEF Kim Shinners
PRODUCTION MANAGER Pamela Loos
ART DIRECTOR Sara Davis
DIRECTOR OF PHOTOGRAPHY Judy L. Hasday
SENIOR PRODUCTION EDITOR J. Christopher Higgins

STAFF FOR *THE HORSE IN HARNESS*

EDITOR Sally Cheney
ASSOCIATE ART DIRECTOR Takeshi Takahashi
SERIES DESIGNER Keith Trego

CHESTNUT PRODUCTIONS AND CHOPTANK SYNDICATE, INC.

EDITORIAL AND PICTURE RESEARCH Mary Hull and Norman Macht
LAYOUT AND PRODUCTION Lisa Hochstein

http://www.chelseahouse.com

First Printing

1 3 5 7 9 8 6 4 2

Library of Congress Cataloguing-in-Publication Data Applied For.

Horse Library SET: 0-7910-6650-9
The Horse in Harness: 0-7910-6658-4

TABLE OF CONTENTS

This Roman mosaic shows a chariot racer with a team of four horses competing in a colosseum, in which there are also gladiators and wild beasts.

HORSE POWER

Less than 100 years ago the horse was the most efficient and reliable means of transportation known to man. Throughout history, horses in harness have been used in war, business, agriculture, and public and private transportation, as well as sport and recreation. Before there were automobiles, tractors, and trucks, horses in harness hauled freight and transported goods; horses tugged streetcars in the nation's cities; horses drove families to church on Sunday; horses brought steam-powered fire engines to the scenes of fires; horses pulled plows through the heavy soil, and these same horses later drove the resulting crops to market.

The harnessing of the horse is directly tied to the rise of civilization. Harnessing a horse to a plow and harrow, a cultivating tool that smooths soil and prepares it for planting, made it possible for ancient peoples to increase their agricultural production, because a horse's strength and endurance was vastly greater than that of a human. Horses also made human migration easier. Unlike an ox, which can travel only about four miles a day, horses can cover twenty miles or more a day while pulling a heavy load.

Human beings have a long relationship with the horse. The first contact between horses and humans was among Cro-Magnon people, who hunted horses for their meat, killing them by chasing them off cliffs. Prehistoric cave paintings discovered in the Lascaux Cave in Dordogne, France, tell the story of these hunts, which left as many as 10,000 horse skeletons at the bottom of a single cliff.

It was not long before humans learned to harness the power of the horse for work and warfare. Between 3000 and 4000 B.C., nomadic peoples living on the steppes of Central Asia domesticated horses. They raised them for their meat and milk and used them as pack animals and mounts. The nomadic peoples of Eastern Europe and Southern Russia may have been the first to use bits and bridles on horses, as there is evidence of rawhide and rope bits being used by these tribes as early as 4000 B.C.

The mythology of many cultures includes the horse in harness. Horses pulled the flaming chariot of the Indian sun god, Indra, across the sky. The Greek god of the sea, Poseidon, was pulled through the water by hippo-like horses.

A circa 2500 B.C. coin from the city of Ur in Mesopotamia depicts a team of four horses yoked to a cart like oxen and controlled through the use of a nose ring, rather than a bit and reins. For a long time, humans used yokes,

A border from a Greek vase, circa 500–450 B.C., depicts soldiers and charioteers in combat.

wooden frames that join draft animals at the head or neck, on horses; but the anatomy of the horse is different from that of an ox. The yoke cut into the horse's windpipe, restricting its ability to breathe, especially when pulling heavy loads. Eventually, a better system of harnessing, unique to horses, was invented. By 300 B.C., the Chinese had begun using a breast strap harness on horses, although this technique did not arrive in the west until much later. By stepping forward into the breast strap harness, the horse's pushing action created a pulling effect through the harness traces, which tugged on the load. With nothing to restrict its wind, the horse could pull a much heavier load than before.

By 3000 B.C., horses were pulling Mesopotamian war chariots. Ancient Egyptian, Assyrian, Greek, and Roman art depicts horses pulling chariots for warfare and sport. Clay tablets engraved in cuneiform script in 1400 B.C. provide instructions for the selection, training, and conditioning of chariot horses for warfare.

Xenophon, a Greek horseman who lived circa 400 B.C., wrote *The Art of Horsemanship*, one of the earliest treatises

In a scene from an Etruscan tomb, a chariot racer with two horses competes in the biga, a two-horse chariot race, circa 500 B.C. Note that the horses appear to be harnessed at the neck with a type of yoke.

on horses. He believed that the horse, a naturally timid animal, must be made bold so that it could excel on the battlefield. Xenophon's exercises for acclimating horses to unusual sounds and sights included walking the horse through public streets and marketplaces until it was no longer afraid of noise and people. Xenophon also believed that the horse responded better to kind ways than harsh ones, and that a mutual trust had to be established between the horse and its master.

Chariot Racing

The sport of chariot racing was popular among the Etruscans and Greeks, who introduced the four-horse chariot race, or quadriga, to the Olympics in 680 B.C. The two-horse chariot race, or biga, was added in 408 B.C. In these races, teams of charioteers stood erect in highly decorated and lightweight chariots. One racer would drive the horses while the other shot arrows. Blades were attached to the axles of the chariot wheels, and when the chariots collided, men and horses were sometimes slashed by the blades.

One of the most popular spots for Roman chariot racing was the Circus Maximus, which could hold 250,000 spectators, roughly one-fourth of the population of Rome. Teams of four, six, eight, or even 12 chariot racers competed in the ring at the same time, racing the equivalent of four miles over seven laps of the Circus.

Rome had four chariot racing companies, each identified

Team Loyalty

Nearly 2,000 years ago the Roman scholar Pliny wrote of the passion his fellow Romans felt for their favorite chariot racing teams:

"I am the more astonished that so many thousands of grown men should be possessed again and again with a childish passion to look at galloping horses, and men standing upright in their chariots. If, indeed, they were attracted by the swiftness of the horses or the skill of the men, one could account for this enthusiasm. But in fact it is a bit of cloth they favour, a bit of cloth that captivates them. And if during the running the racers were to exchange colours, their partisans would change sides, and instantly forsake the very drivers and horses whom they were just before recognizing from afar, and clamorously saluting by name."

by the color of the tunics worn by the racers—green, red, yellow, and blue—much as jockeys are recognized by their racing silks today. Spectators rooted for their favorite color just as fans root for sports teams today. Although public gambling was not allowed, private betting on chariot races was widespread, and Roman bookmakers used carrier pigeons to deliver the race results to off-track bettors.

The chariot racers were all slaves. If a charioteer was very successful, he might eventually be able to buy his freedom, but many charioteers died young. Rounding the turns of the racetrack at high speed was dangerous, and accidents were common. Charioteers sometimes tied the reins around their bodies so they could use their weight to control the horses. Even if they had knives to cut themselves loose in case of an accident, they could still be dragged or trampled to death. Unlike Roman military chariots, which were quite sturdy, racing chariots were so lightweight they were very unstable and frequently broke apart when hit.

Around 900 A.D., with the invention of horseshoes, horses became faster, more efficient work animals. But it was not until 1000 A.D., with the invention of the horse collar in Europe, that horses became the preferred beast of burden. This new horse collar rested on the animal's shoulders. It was superior to either a yoke or breast strap harness in that it maximized the power of the horse. The revolutionary effect this new harness had on horsepower cannot be underestimated. Horses now surpassed oxen and other beasts of burden in agricultural use.

The invention of the horse collar, together with the invention of a heavier plow, transformed agriculture during the Middle Ages. Feudal lords supplied horses to their tenant farmers, who sometimes hitched two horses together to pull the new heavier plow and make a deeper furrow than was previously possible. Better plowing and a more efficient use of horses resulted in greater agricultural yields than had ever been known. The increase in the food supply made the growth of new cities possible. More people had an agricultural surplus which they could trade at market. Since there was enough food to go around, not everyone was needed to farm; some people could live in cities and engage in other occupations. The labor of horses made so much possible for so many.

Horses were used extensively for warfare during the Middle Ages, and they were bred for specific purposes. Heavy draft breeds, the ancestors of today's Belgian and Percheron horses, were popular mounts for knights in battle. Known as "destriers," these war horses could carry a greater load, and their extra weight gave a greater impact to the knight's lance when he charged. Sometimes these war horses wore iron-spiked shoes so they could trample men with great effectiveness. The destriers were also popular as tournament horses for jousting and other sporting events.

Horses had an impact on the New World as well. After the Spanish conquistadors brought horses to the Americas in the early 1500s, the Plains Indians developed a horse culture. They used horses to hunt buffalo and bison, and to drag loads on a travois (*trav-wah*), a wheel-less horse-drawn vehicle attached to the horse by two poles. The Plains Indians also used horses to help them in their wars with other tribes. Horses gave them speed and mobility. The wild Mustangs that live in the American west today are the ancestors of these Indian horses.

European armies used the horse to mobilize their artillery as well as their cavalry. The 17th century Swedish king Gustavus Adolphus, who led Protestant armies into Germany during the Thirty Years War with the Holy Roman Empire, used the horse in new ways to create a more efficient military. Instead of using a team of horses to pull heavy artillery, Gustavus commissioned lighter cannons, and he hitched a single horse to each one, so that they could be moved faster and more efficiently. These mobile cannons played a huge role in Gustavus's victories at Breitenfeld in 1631 and Lutzen in 1632, where he was killed.

While the horse had long been used for war and agriculture, forms of mass horse-drawn transportation did not develop until the advent of good roads. A horse-drawn cart or carriage was not practical or comfortable unless driven on a sufficiently wide and smooth path. At first wagons and carts could move easily only within cities. For longer trips to places where the roads were poor, people rode horseback.

With the improvement of the roads in Europe in the 1600s, horse-drawn transportation flourished. The royalty of Europe first made coaches fashionable. Ornate, sometimes gilded coaches carried kings and queens on state visits. The horses that pulled these heavy and ornate

How a Horse Brakes a Load

A horse brakes a load with the help of its harness. The breeching (pronounced britching) strap on a driving harness is a heavy leather strap that wraps around a horse's hindquarters below the tail. Together with the rest of the harness and cart, it works as a braking and backing system. The breeching remains loose on the horse's hindquarters until the horse backs up or restrains the load, at which point it pushes against the horse's hindquarters. The horse uses its weight and power to stop the load against its haunches.

carriages had to be strong, but fashionable. Fancy high-stepping carriage horses that matched in size, color, and gait were bred for coach use.

While fancy carriages were the privilege of the wealthy, ordinary people also benefited from improvements to the road system. In 1706 the first stagecoach service began operating between York and London, England. The stage-coach was named for the way it stopped at designated points, or stages, along its scheduled route. Stage stops were typically 15–20 miles apart and each stop had an inn where travelers could eat, drink, and sleep. Stagecoach drivers might change at these stops, and tired horses were exchanged for fresh ones. Stagecoaches were generally pulled by four horses. The two faster, lighter horses were placed at the lead of the hitch, where they set the pace for the two rear horses. Heavier horses were placed in the rear. Known as "wheelers," because they were placed closest to the wheels of the coach, these horses were the brakes of the coach, as their haunches had to slow the weight of the vehicle when it descended hills. If the wheelers could not brake a fully loaded stagecoach on a downward slope, the coach could roll out of control, so good wheelers were very important to the safety of the passengers.

Early stagecoaches, even those suspended by leather straps, were uncomfortably bouncy, because the roads were not well maintained. After 1750, turnpikes began to be built in England, and though these roads charged a fee for vehicles, they were well maintained and easy to travel. When roads in England improved to the point where driving became a pleasurable pastime, four-wheeled vehicles known as phaetons came into popular use. In 1784 mail delivery coaches began regular travel in England. The average mail coach horse was put to such hard use that it

In the 19th and early 20th centuries, before there were buses and subways, horse- or mule-drawn streetcars provided inner-city transportation. This streetcar operated in Cowley County, Kansas.

survived only three years. By 1840, when the railroad began to link most areas of the country together, stage-coaches fell out of use in England.

Long after the railroad supplanted the stagecoach in Europe and the United States, the horse and buggy persisted in rural and urban areas. Horses were still the primary means of short-haul transportation, whether taking the doctor on a house call or hauling freight between businesses in the city. Horse-drawn transportation was essential to business and industry. In the United States, the American

Tin Lizzies

Before the advent of the automobile in the United States, families relied on a driving horse for transportation. Every town and city had watering troughs for horses, and their locations were marked on maps. Hitching posts and mounting blocks were a common sight. In the early twentieth century Lizzie was one of the most popular names for the family mare, so the first automobiles became known, jokingly, as "tin Lizzies."

Express Company used horses to pull its delivery wagons. In 1912, even though it had begun using automobiles, American Express still had 1,300 horses in service.

When the horse was the primary means of transportation, much attention was given to the breeding of horses and the creation of different types of horses for different purposes. Horses were bred for specific functions such as speed or power, or grace in harness. Just as we have jeeps and station wagons and racecars today, we have breeds of horses for such different purposes as driving, farm work, and racing.

Whatever its breeding, a driving horse must trust its driver and act sensibly when it encounters traffic and other obstacles on the road or in the field.

2

POPULAR BREEDS OF HARNESS HORSES

While almost any breed of horse can be harnessed and trained to pull a carriage or wagon, some horses have been bred for specific harness functions. Trotters and pacers are bred for harness racing; draft breeds are well suited to heavy work and agricultural labor; fancy high-stepping breeds make elegant driving horses. This chapter covers some of the most popular breeds for driving, show, work, and harness racing.

The Hackney

Because of its high-stepping trotting action and graceful look, the Hackney is a popular harness and carriage horse for shows and competitions. Called "the ballerina of the show ring," the Hackney horse was bred to be a high stepper and is known for the way it picks its forelegs up high and thrusts its feet forward, making a rounded step. The Hackney takes its name from the old French word "haquenee," which referred to any horse with an especially comfortable trot. Eventually the term "hackney" came to refer to any horse, ridden or driven, with a good trot and great stamina.

The modern breed of Hackney was developed in England in the 18th century when breeders crossed Arabians with English trotters like the Norfolk Roadster. It was a time when trotters were in demand. Previously, a heavier horse was needed to pull a load because the country's roads were so poor they were often full of deep ruts. But with improvements to the road system, it became possible to travel at greater speed. Fast trotting horses came into demand. The hackney was considered "the ultimate driving horse of the 1880s" and in 1883 the first official Hackney breed registry was established in England. Hackneys almost disappeared when the advent of trains, and then automobiles, led to a decline in the need for driving horses, but a few dedicated breeders kept the Hackney alive.

The Hackney is a high-spirited horse with a raised head and alert look. It stands 14 hands and taller. (A horse's height is measured in hands. One hand equals four inches.) A Hackney pony measuring under 14 hands was developed in the 19th century. Hackney horses and ponies are bay, dark brown, black, or chestnut.

Haflinger

The Haflinger was named for the village of Hafling in the Tyrolean Alps. This hardy, dependable breed hails from the

Tyrolean mountains of Austria and Northern Italy, where they provided surefooted transportation on the steep narrow paths between mountain villages. The Haflinger is chestnut in color with a light, often pure white, mane and tail. Their average height is between 13.2 and 14.3 hands. Known for their willingness to work, their surprising strength, and their versatility, the Haflinger is a popular breed for draft work and driving, as well as endurance riding, dressage, jumping, and trail riding. Because of its good nature, the Haflinger is also used in therapeutic riding programs.

A team of Haflingers negotiates a water obstacle during the cross-country phase of a combined driving event. Haflingers are known for being hardy and sure footed.

The American Standardbred

Standardbreds are the world's fastest trotters and pacers and they are used largely, but not exclusively, for harness racing. The breed was founded with an English Thoroughbred named Messenger, who was brought to the United States in 1788. Messenger's great grandson Hambletonian 10, born in 1849, was another founding sire of the breed. He was so popular that all modern Standardbreds can trace their ancestry to him. As trotting races grew in popularity, the breed was refined in order to develop a superior racehorse.

The name "Standardbred" originated in 1879, when it was used to refer to those trotting horses who could go a mile at a standard speed of 2 minutes and 30 seconds or better. Only the trotters who met this criterion were allowed into the breed registry. Today the standard time for a two-year-old Standardbred to trot a mile is 2.20, and for three year-olds it is 2.15. Many Standardbreds are even faster, and some, like the famous pacer Dan Patch, can cover a mile in 1.55 or better. The Standardbred is not as tall as the Thoroughbred but tends to be longer, with strong legs and powerful hindquarters that provide the forward thrust necessary for the trot or pace. A Standardbred has a larger head than a Thoroughbred, and may even have a Roman nose. The height of a Standardbred ranges from 14.2 to 17.2 hands, although the average is 15.2 hands. They generally weigh between 900 and 1200 pounds. The dominant colors are bay, brown, and black.

Standardbreds are either trotters or pacers, and their gait is largely determined by pedigree. Trotters move their legs in diagonal pairs, and the propulsion comes from the opposite front and hind legs. For example, when the trotter's right front leg moves forward, so does its left hind leg.

Pacers, however, move their legs in lateral pairs, much like a camel. When a pacer's right front leg moves forward, so does its right hind leg. Pacers are also known as "side-wheelers." Pacers are faster than trotters, and they are less likely to break stride. Today pacers make up 80 percent of all harness racing horses.

In addition to making champion trotters and pacers, Standardbreds are steady mounts and driving horses. They are known for having bombproof temperaments.

The Amish are one of the few groups in the United States today who continue to rely on horses as a primary means of transportation. They use Standardbreds as driving horses because of their speed, stamina, and trustworthiness. While the Amish rely on draft breeds like the Belgian and Percheron for farm work, Amish buggies are often pulled by Standardbreds, many of them retired harness racers.

The Russian Trotter

The Orlov Trotter was bred by Count Orlov at his farm in Russia in the late 1700s. The breed was famous for its powerful trotting, and it was a popular carriage horse and harness racehorse, although it was not as fast as the American Standardbred. Orlov Trotters frequently lost to American Standardbreds on European racetracks. As a result, Standardbred stallions were bred with Orlov Trotter mares to create a faster horse. This cross, known as the Russian Trotter, was a faster, lighter horse with less stamina. After the Russian Revolution of 1917, the Russian Trotter was relegated to agricultural work and army transport. In 1949 it became recognized as a distinct breed. The Russian Trotter looks very similar to the American Standardbred. Its dominant colors are gray and black, although chestnut and bay also occur.

Lisa Singer drives her team of Morgans around a sand obstacle at the 1995 USET Festival of Champions. The Morgan horse is known for its upright neck, which gives it a refined bearing. The Morgan is a versatile horse that excels at riding, driving, and endurance competition.

The Morgan

With their upright necks, expressive eyes, small ears, and proud bearing, Morgan horses are easily identified. Known for their sweet temperaments, Morgans are also prized for their versatility. The Morgan breed was sired by a bay stallion named Figure, who was owned by Justin Morgan of Springfield, Massachusetts, and Randolph, Vermont. Faster and stronger than other horses, Figure was equally at ease pulling a plow or a buggy. No other horse ever beat him in a race. Figure had stamina and power, but he was also agile and fast. He was an easy keeper and did not need a lot of food to maintain his weight. Because it was so unusual to find all of these qualities in one horse, Figure became in demand as a stud, and his progeny became known as Morgan horses. By the mid-19th century Morgans were highly sought after as general-purpose horses for both work and pleasure. Morgans were used as cavalry horses during the Civil War, and they have also been used by U.S. Parks Service rangers as surefooted trail mounts and packhorses.

The Morgan averages between 14.1 and 15.2 hands, and can be bay, black, brown, chestnut, buckskin, cream, gray,

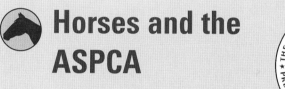 

Horses and the ASPCA

The American Society for the Prevention of Cruelty to Animals (ASPCA), the oldest animal protection organization in the western hemisphere, was founded in 1866 by Henry Bergh, who was appalled by the mistreatment of the harness horses he saw in New York City. Determined to do something to help these poor animals, which included the city's overworked trolley horses, Bergh helped pass the first law to protect animals in the United States. The ASPCA also opened the first animal clinic to rescue injured horses and rehabilitate them. This clinic was the first in the country to use anesthesia in animal surgery. The original seal of the ASPCA, designed by noted illustrator Frank Leslie, depicts an angel protecting a poor cart horse that has collapsed from exhaustion and is being beaten by its driver.

dun, or palomino in color. The Morgan is one of the most common breeds shown at combined driving and carriage events and is also popular in park harness classes, which showcase its high action.

The American Miniature

The American Miniature is a scaled-down version of a large-size horse. Miniatures were originally bred in Europe as pets for the nobility, although some were also put to work hauling carts in coal mines. The American Miniature

The American Miniature is no taller than 34 inches at the withers, but it is not a pony.

is so small that only the tiniest child can ride it, but it enjoys great popularity as a carriage horse. Miniatures are shown in a variety of driving classes, including multiple-hitch, roadster driving, obstacle driving, single pleasure driving, and fine viceroy, a fancy carriage class. Any color or marking pattern is acceptable, as is any eye color. The primary criterion is height, which cannot exceed 34 inches at the withers.

The Cleveland Bay

The Cleveland Bay is the oldest breed of English horse, and it is the last pure warmblood breed. It takes its name from the Cleveland region of northeast England and its bay color. The Cleveland Bay's ancestors were pack horses bred by the monasteries of England to transport goods. These hardy pack horses were later crossed with Barb horses to produce a superior horse known as the Cleveland Bay.

The Cleveland Bay's speed, power, and style made it one of England's most popular carriage horses. The breed has a natural jumping ability as well, so it became a popular hunter. An official Cleveland Bay breed registry was begun in England in 1884. The Cleveland Bay averages about 16 hands and 1,225–1,500 pounds. Its color is always bay with black points on the mane, tail, and legs. Cleveland Bays are known for their longevity. According to the *Guiness Book of World Records*, the oldest horse on record—a Cleveland Bay—lived to be 62 years old.

Because of its versatility, the Cleveland Bay has been crossed extensively with numerous breeds to create powerful hunter/jumpers and graceful carriage horses. In 18th century England the Cleveland Bay was crossed with Thoroughbreds to create a very fashionable and tall carriage horse known as the Yorkshire coach horse. Many European warmbloods,

Holsteiner geldings driven by USET driver Elizabeth Chesson encounter trees during the cross-country phase of a pairs combined driving event. Holsteiners are one of the oldest German breeds.

including the Hanoverian, Holstein, and Oldenburg, owe much of their jumping ability to Cleveland Bay blood. The demand for the Cleveland Bay was very high in the 1880s, and it was exported to several continents.

Because of its strength and sensible temperament, the Cleveland Bay was used as an artillery horse during World War I and as a police horse. Although the Cleveland Bay declined in numbers after the advent of the automobile, it has always held a special place in England. The Queen of England continues to keep Cleveland Bays in her stable, and they are used to pull royal coaches and carriages. Worldwide, however, there are fewer than 500 purebred Cleveland Bays, making them an endangered breed.

The Norwegian Fjord

The Norwegian Fjord is one of the oldest and most primitive breeds of horses. The Norwegian Fjord closely resembles the Ice Age horses depicted in ancient cave paintings over 30,000 years ago, and it is the only horse to retain such primitive markings as zebra stripes on the legs, a dorsal stripe down the back, and a black stripe of mane hair in the center of a white mane. Norwegian Fjords were first domesticated around 2000 B.C., and the Vikings may have ridden these sturdy horses as war mounts. Norwegian Fjords are believed to have contributed to the development of several British pony breeds as well as the Icelandic pony.

Norwegian Fjords have been used for agricultural work in Norway for centuries, and they continue to be used for draft work today. They are known for their strength, stamina, and gentleness. Norwegian Fjords have a short, compact body and round chest, as well as an extra-thick coat that helps them survive harsh winters. Their average height is 13.2 to 15 hands, and their average weight is 900–1,200 pounds. The majority of Norwegian Fjords are a brown dun color, but other colors, including red dun, grey, pale dun, gold, and yellow dun, also occur.

Today Norwegian Fjords are used for draft work, driving, and riding, including therapeutic riding. In 1994 Norwegian Fjords were used at the Lillehammer, Norway, Olympics to drive Olympic contenders and other celebrities to and from Olympic venues.

The Suffolk

The oldest English breed of heavy horse is the Suffolk, also known as the Suffolk Punch, a horse once described as "barrel-shaped with not much daylight under." Short-legged and stout, the Suffolk is the only draft breed that was bred exclusively as a plow horse. As early as 1506, farmers in eastern England bred the Suffolk to drag a plow through the heavy clay soil of their region. The Suffolk has no feathering on its legs, as that is impractical for a horse that was designed to spend its time in muddy clay. The average height of a Suffolk is between 15.1 and 16.2 hands, and they typically weigh between 1,980 and 2,200 pounds. The Suffolk is always a chestnut color, although there are many shade variations. The Suffolk is lower to the ground than other draft breeds, making it is easier to harness and trailer.

The Shire

One of the largest horses in the world, the Shire takes its name from the shires, or counties, of England. Originally bred as an English warhorse, the Shire was admired by Roman soldiers, who marveled at its strength and courage. Later the Shire was used to pull heavy wagons in the cities. On poorly maintained early roads, the Shire could pull even the heaviest of loads out of a rut. In the 19th century, England exported Shires to U.S. cities and farms where they pulled street cars and heavy wagons and plowed fields. The first Shire breed registry was formed in the U.S. in 1885. Like the other draft breeds, Shires were largely replaced by trucks and tractors after World War I, and by the 1980s the number of Shires in the U.S. had dwindled to just 121. Although the worldwide population of Shires is still small, today they are making a comeback, thanks to their popularity at draft horse shows.

The Shire is a popular dray horse, and English brewers like to use Shires to pull their beer wagons. The Shire also continues to be used for agricultural work. Though their average height ranges from 16.2 to 17.2, Shires can be as tall as 19 hands. The average Shire weighs one ton and can move a five ton load. The Shire is characterized by its long legs, which have extensive feathering. Dominant colors are black, brown, grey, and bay.

The Clydesdale

One of the most recognizable of the draft breeds, the Clydesdale is a large horse that takes its name from the River Clyde in the region of Lanarkshire, Scotland. Clydesdales were bred for hauling coal and for agricultural work. They were also used as carriage horses.

The Clydesdale, one of the largest draft breeds, is known for its feathered feet and high-stepping action.

The Clydesdale has long legs with white feathering, and is usually black, bay (reddish brown), brown, roan (red, black, or brown undercolor, with lighter hair interspersed throughout), or chestnut in color, often with white points on the legs and face. They are quite agile, despite the fact that they often weigh 2,000 pounds or more. The Clydesdale has relatively high action for a draft breed, and it picks its feet up cleanly at every step with no scuffing. They were exported from Scotland to all parts of the world, and they continue to be popular hitch horses in the United States, where there are 2,500–3,000 of them. The largest Clydesdale herd in the world today is maintained by the Anheuser-Busch company, which has between 225 and 250 horses.

The Belgian

The Belgian horse descends from the warhorses of medieval times who carried knights into battle. They are the most direct descendants of the ancient "black horse of Flanders," which provided the foundation for all modern draft breeds. Belgium exported the breed extensively, and though they did not catch on in this country immediately, today they are more Belgian horses in the United States than all other breeds of draft horses combined.

With short muscular legs and a barrel chest, the Belgian is a compact, sturdy horse with tremendous power. The average Belgian stands 16 to 18 hands high and weighs 1,800–2,000 pounds or more. Because they are hard workers and easy keepers, Belgians are popular horses for farm work, logging, and sleigh and hay rides. Many Amish communities use Belgian horses to pull farm machinery. The dominant color for the Belgian in the United States is chestnut, with a white mane and tail and white points.

Belgians are a popular hitch horse and are frequently seen at country fairs and draft horse competitions, either as carriage horses, as part of a multiple-horse hitch, or as pulling horses. Belgians, like many other draft horses, have also been crossbred with performance horses like the Thoroughbred to create a powerful warmblood with great size and athletic ability and a gentle, willing temperament.

The Percheron

The Percheron originated in the region of La Perche, France, when heavy draft mares like the Boulonais were bred with Arab stallions. Percherons are either black or grey and they average 16.2–17.3 hands and 1,900 pounds and up in weight. Between 1850 and 1941, Percherons were widely imported into the United States for farm work and to haul freight in cities. Before the advent of trucks and tractors, they were one of the most popular draft breeds in the United States. After World War II, the Percheron began to disappear, except in a few rural places, including Amish communities who continued to breed Percherons for farm work. Today they are popular in competition hitching and carriage classes, and they can be seen pulling carts in places like Central Park, New York.

George Bowman Sr. of
Great Britain successfully
negotiates a wooden bridge
with a well-matched team
of Cumberland Cob geldings
at the 1998 World Equestrian
Games in Italy.

DRIVING

U nlike riders, drivers sit far behind their horses. They cannot use subtle body pressure or leg cues to communicate to the horse or horses. Instead they rely on a combination of rein tension, voice cues, and whip cues. A driving horse must be sound, well-conditioned, and sensible. The driving horse must be able to encounter traffic and other hazards without shying or running away. When hitched to other horses, a driving horse must also be able to work as a member of a team.

Unlike riding, driving is a sport for almost any age or fitness level. People who are too old to ride can still drive. In some cases, horses that are too old to be ridden can still be driven, as driving puts less stress on a horse's knees than riding. People with physical handicaps that prevent them from riding may be able to enjoy horses through driving. All types of ponies and horses are suited to driving. Miniature horses that are too small to be ridden can be enjoyed as driving animals.

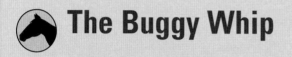

The Buggy Whip

Buggy whip manufacturing was an important 19th century industry that has become virtually obsolete today. As a result, the buggy whip became a metaphor for outmoded technology. Today, companies worry that their product will come the "buggy whip" of the 21st century. But, at its peak, 20 million buggy whips were manufactured each year. In 1910, for example, there were 80,000 automobiles manufactured in the United States and 1,750,000 horse drawn vehicles. The United States Whip Manufacturing Company of Westfield, Massachusetts, the largest whip maker in the world, once churned out 25,000 whips a day. The city of Westfield, known as Whip City, boasted almost 40 whip-manufacturing companies that produced 18 million whips annually—90 percent of the world's supply. Whips were frequently made from a rawhide base that was covered in rattan, then glued, tapered, and braided with silk or cotton thread.

In 1911, the U.S. Whip Company used 600 tons of rattan (a type of Asian grass); 185,000 pounds of hides; 75 tons of thread; 300,000 yards of cotton cloth; 100 tons of iron (for the butts of higher quality whips); 75 carloads of wood (for the butts of cheaper whips); and 18,000 gallons of varnish to make whips. Over 200 kinds of whips were available, from the very expensive to the very inexpensive, including buggy whips, four-in-hand whips, track whips, cab whips, express whips, team whips, stage stalks, riding and hunting crops, and jockey whips.

Sem Groenewoud has won four USET Four-in-Hand Driving Championships with his Dutch Warmblood horses. The passengers in the back of his cart shift their weight to help balance the vehicle during sharp turns.

Before it is hitched to a vehicle, a driving horse is trained on the ground. An important part of this training is getting the horse accustomed to all kinds of strange noises, sights, and sensations. Called "sacking out," this phase of training teaches the horse not to be afraid of umbrellas, flapping plastic bags, traffic, bicycles, and all kinds of potentially scary situations that might be encountered on the road, especially if the horse is going to work in traffic or attend parades or horse shows. The horse is also slowly taught to accept a harness. Driving harnesses frequently use blinders on the bridle to prevent the horse from seeing behind and catching a glimpse of the cart. Blinders focus the horse's vision ahead.

Before it is hitched to a vehicle for the first time, a horse is "ground driven." The trainer holds the reins and walks behind the horse, teaching it to go forward and backward, turn left and right, and stop on command. The driver must have good hands and be able to keep an even tension on the horse's mouth without developing a "belly," or slack, in the reins. Too much tension spoils a horse's mouth, while too little tension will confuse the horse.

The term "gee" is used to tell the horse to go to the right, and the term "haw" is used to tell the horse to bear left. Like the other voice cues, these signals are used in conjunction with the reins to convey a message to the horse. Once the horse has learned to obey these cues while being ground driven, the trainer goes to the next step, hitching the horse to a training vehicle.

 **Jingle Bells**

The purpose of harness bells, which used to be required by law in many areas (just as a horn is required on cars today), was to alert others to the presence of a horse and driver and prevent accidents. A collision of two teams hauling passengers or heavy loads could be fatal, and on narrow paths and at intersections, harness bells served a useful purpose. The bells were especially important in winter as a horse and sleigh sliding along in the snow made very little noise. So when you think of bells on Bobtail ringing, keep in mind that those bells are there to alert pedestrians and other drivers to the presence of an oncoming vehicle.

A simple two-wheeled cart is often used as a training vehicle. The cart has two poles, or shafts, on either side, and the horse stands between the shafts, which are tied into the harness. The cart is further connected to the horse by the singletree, the bar to which the horse's harness traces are hooked. When the horse pushes forward into its breast strap or collar, its push creates a pulling effect on the cart by means of the harness, and the cart is tugged along behind the horse.

While driving was a necessity until the last century, driving also has a long history as a pleasurable pastime in the United States. In the 19th century American driving enthusiasts formed coaching clubs and went on drives in the city and country, packing picnic lunches and walking sticks for these afternoons of leisure. One of the most famous coaching clubs was the Four in Hand Club of New York, whose members drove coaches pulled by teams of four horses. The New York Coaching Club sponsored a parade each year in which elegant coaches were drawn up and down Fifth Avenue and club members wore the fancy club uniform: a bottle green coat with brass buttons and a white top hat.

Carriage driving has never gone out of style. It continues to be a popular hobby, and today there are over one hundred driving clubs in the United States. One of the largest is the American Driving Society (ADS), which promotes driving for pleasure and sport. The ADS is the governing body for pleasure driving, combined driving, and driven dressage competitions in the United States, and it works to educate the public about driving methods and safety.

State and county fairs, as well as farm shows, are good places to watch driving events. Among the different driving shows are classes like ladies' single cart and men's single cart, as well as multiple-hitch classes. One of the most popular driving competitions is a multi-phase sport known as combined driving.

The sport of combined driving began in 1968 with the encouragement of Prince Philip of England, who competed in some of the earliest English competitions with his team of Fell ponies. Since then it has grown in popularity and is now officially recognized as one of the United States Equestrian Team (USET) disciplines. Each year USET hosts the National Pairs Driving Championship at its Gladstone Equestrian Center in Gladstone, New Jersey. Combined driving is a three-phase event that is held over the course of one, two, or three days. There are many different levels in combined driving, from beginner to advanced, and drivers compete against other people at their level. Drivers can compete with one horse (single), two horses (called a pair), or four horses (known as four-in-hand). Combined driving is also a multi-breed event. Any size, shape, or breed of horse can be used in competition.

The first phase of combined driving competition is the dressage event, which can best be described as elegance in harness. Initial marks for this event are based on the presentation of the driver and horse(s), and the appearance of the harness and vehicle, which have been carefully polished and shined up for the event. Horses are also judged on their appearance and bearing. Then the dressage test begins. The driver and horse(s) must perform a number of compulsory moves, while the judges watch to see how supple the horse is, how even its paces are, and how rhythmic its steps. In the case of teams or multiple hitches, horses are also judged on how well they work in harmony with each other. Their paces must be evenly matched and they must work in step.

In the cross-country phase of a combined driving competition horses negotiate a complex course that requires them to pass between obstacles with speed and precision.

The second phase in a combined driving competition is a grueling 9–13.5 mile cross-country timed event known as the marathon, which leads horse and driver over roads and fields. The marathon tests the driver's skill and judgment as well as the stamina of the horses. The course is divided into sections that are negotiated at either the walk or trot, and drivers must keep up the speed specified for each section or they lose points. The final section of the course contains up to eight natural and artificial obstacles that must be negotiated at speed, including water hazards, trees,

During the cones competition, horses must move with precision to avoid knocking the balls off the cones, which are set just inches wider than the wheel tracks of the carriage.

sharp turns, uneven ground, and gates. The horse must have tremendous trust in the driver and not be afraid of the obstacles, even though it encounters them at speed. The driver must maintain control at all times and decide the fastest way to negotiate each obstacle. For this event, the driver is allowed to bring a navigator aboard to help. The navigator sits in the back of the vehicle and shifts his or her weight around to help keep the vehicle upright during sharp turns. Drivers and navigators wear helmets and generally use specially designed marathon vehicles, that have four wheels and are equipped with brakes.

The third and final phase of combined driving competition is called the cone, or obstacle course. Horses must recover from the excitement of the marathon phase to concentrate on this exacting course, in which horse and driver work against the clock while executing tight turns and negotiating narrow paths between lines of traffic cones set around a complex course. Balls are set on top of the cones, and if the cones are even slightly bumped, the balls will fall. Obstacles such as flapping fabric, designed to test a horse's bravery and its trust in the driver, are placed around the course. A horse must be very disciplined to pass through the course without knocking over any of the cones. At the advanced level, the cones are set only ten inches wider than the wheel tracks of the vehicle. The cones test the horse's obedience to the driver, and the driver's skill in handling the reins.

The winner of a combined driving event is the horse and driver team with the fastest time and the lowest number of penalty points. Among the most famous combined driving competitions are the International Grand Prix, held in May of each year at the Royal Windsor Horse Show in England, and the Nation's Cup, held each summer in Aachen, Germany.

In harness racing there are pacers and trotters; this horse is a pacer or "sidewheeler" because he moves the legs on one side of his body in tandem. He is also wearing plastic loops called hobbles, which help keep his legs moving in sync.

HARNESS RACING

In the days of the Puritans, horse racing was prohibited in New England, but trotting was not, so horse owners frequently engaged in trotting races to compare the speed of their horses. Most of these races were harness races. Harness racing grew to be a very popular pastime among Americans at racetracks, county fairs, and agricultural fairs. Today harness racing attracts 30 million people a year in the United States.

In harness racing, a Standardbred horse pulls a light two-wheeled vehicle called a sulky around a track at a trot or a pace. The horse must maintain its gait and is not allowed to break into a canter or gallop. The horse with the fastest time wins the race. There are two types of harness racers: trotters and pacers. Whether a horse will be a trotter or pacer is determined by breeding, as the gait is bred into the horse. While pacers move both legs on one side of the body at the same time, trotters move opposite hind and forelegs at the same time. Pacers are believed to descend from a New England breed of saddle horse known as the Narragansett Pacer, which disappeared around 1850. Pacers were most popular in the Midwest and South originally, while trotters were dominant in the Northeast. Today, however, pacers make up 80 percent of all harness racehorses.

In one of the first harness races on record, a horse named Yankee trotted a mile in 2 minutes 59 seconds at a track in Harlem, New York, in 1806. The oldest working harness race track in the country, in Goshen, New York, dates to 1838. Today this track is part of the Harness Racing Museum and Hall of Fame.

 Post Position

The post position in which the racehorses start is determined by a draw before the race. Generally, a position close to the inside rail increases the chances of winning. When a horse is placed on the outside, it must either start quickly to get ahead of the inside horses for a good position or lag behind on the rail to avoid having to race on the outside. A horse racing on the outside of a track must travel a greater distance than the inside horses and so loses ground on every turn. Harness racing horses wear numbers on their heads and on their racing silks so they can be identified at a distance. The number they wear corresponds to their post position.

19th century American lithographers Nathan Currier and James Ives catered to the American obsession with harness racing by mass-producing lithographs like this 1880 picture of the pacer Maud S., known as "The Queen of the Turf."

The Standardbred Horse became an established breed in 1879, and membership in the breed registry was based on a horse's ability to go a mile in at least 2 minutes and 30 seconds. Popular 19th and early 20th century harness racers included Maud S.; Flora Temple, the bob-tailed mare featured in the song "Camptown Races"; Star Pointer, who in 1897 became the first pacer to make a two minute mile; and Dan Patch, a horse so prized he traveled in his own railroad car, who could do a mile in 1 minute 55 seconds. Some of these horses were immortalized by the American lithographers Currier and Ives, who captured the nation's love affair with harness racing in a series of prints featuring the most popular trotters of the day. Many of these prints are on display at the Harness Racing Museum and Hall of Fame.

In 1939 several regional harness racing organizations fused to form a single entity, the United States Trotting Association (USTA). Today the USTA is responsible for setting rules for the sport, insuring the integrity of harness racing, registering horses for breeding and racing, and licensing officials, trainers, drivers, and owners.

In 1940, shortly after the formation of the USTA, harness racing was made even more popular with the introduction of pari-mutuel racing, allowing people at the track to place bets on the races. Pari-mutuel comes from the French and means "to bet amongst ourselves." The first pari-mutuel racing took place at Roosevelt Raceway in New York City. Racing programs for harness races contain information on each of the horses being entered for a race. A horse's previous wins or losses are listed, along with data such as whether or not the horse has broken pace in previous races, and the condition of the track on which the horse raced on a particular day. This information is designed to help bettors determine how likely the horse is to win a given race.

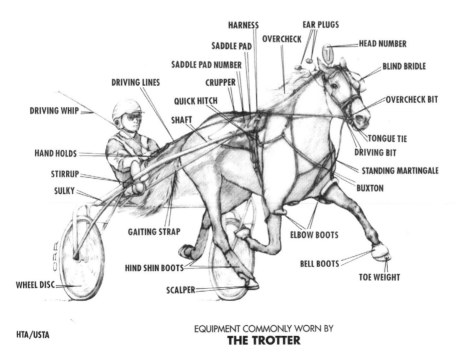

HTA/USTA

EQUIPMENT COMMONLY WORN BY
THE TROTTER

In 1946 Roosevelt Raceway became the first track to use a mobile starting gate, allowing the horses to get an even running start. The mobile starting gate consists of a set of metal wings attached to either side of an automobile that moves slowly around the track at the beginning of a race. After the horses have been warmed up and are ready to race, they run along the track, forming rows of several horses behind the wings. Once the race is underway, the starting gate speeds up and moves off the track.

Although the horses only trot or pace, they travel at high speed and drivers must be skilled at handling the reins in order to keep their horse in the best position at all times. Drivers navigate around slower horses and determine the best and fastest path to the finish line.

Standardbreds begin racing as two- or three-year-olds. They wear a harness and bridle with blinders, as well as a shadow roll, which prevents the horses from being distracted. Trotters and pacers also wear a Buxton martingale, a device that keeps the harness from slipping out of place. Pacers sometimes wear plastic hobbles, which help keep their legs moving in sync and prevent them from breaking into a run, or going "off-stride." Standardbred racehorses also wear knee boots to protect them in case they strike their knees while trotting or pacing.

The top harness racers in the country follow a route known as the Grand Circuit, moving from track to track each week throughout the summer, racing for large cash prizes known as purses. Both pacers and trotters have a Triple Crown, or top three races for the best horses. The pacing Triple Crown consists of the Cane Pace, held at Yonkers Raceway; the Messenger Stakes, held at Ladbroke at the Meadows; and the Little Brown Jug—the top event for pacers—held at the Delaware, Ohio, County Fairgrounds

World champion pacer Jet Laag tears up the track. In harness racing, the horse's legs come close to striking the sulky where the driver sits, and the sulkies have solid wheels to prevent passing horses from getting a leg caught in the spokes.

each year. For trotters, the Triple Crown races are the Hambletonian, which has a purse of $1.2 million and is held at the Meadowlands outside New York City each August; the Yonkers Trot, held at the Yonkers Raceway; and the Kentucky Futurity, held at Lexington's Red Mile in Lexington, Kentucky. One of the newest events in harness racing is the Breeders' Crown, a series of races with different divisions, which boasts over $4 million in purse money.

In 1980 a pacer named Niatross became the first harness horse to break 1:50 when he came in at 1:49 1/5 at his

Lexington time trial. Niatross shattered numerous records during his career, winning 37 of his 39 starts by such great lengths that the racetracks never had to resort to a photo finish. Niatross had record purse earnings for a two-year-old and over his lifetime earned a record $2 million. Niatross was so popular the Breyer company modeled a toy horse after him in 1998.

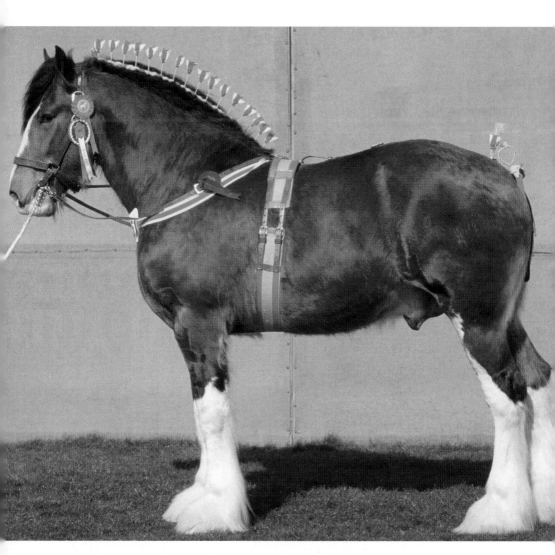

The Shire is the largest of the draft horse breeds. This stallion's mane and tail are braided to show off his muscular neck and hindquarters.

DRAFT HORSES

Draft horses are exceptionally large and strong animals. They developed their distinctive characteristics over thousands of years. During the Pleistocene or Ice Age, the horses roaming in what is today Northern Europe and Scandinavia were cut off from more southern regions by glaciers. Isolated from other horses, they adopted traits that helped them to survive in their cold environment: a heavier body, thicker coat, and ability to survive on minimal food sources. At the end of the Ice Age, heavy horses spread throughout Europe, mixing with other horses, but all modern draft breeds descend from the heavy northern horses of the Ice Age.

A team of four Belgians pull a weighted harrow to prepare a field for planting.

Draft horses take their name from the term draft, which refers to the load-pulling capacity of an animal. Because of their powerful muscles and willing temperaments, draft horses have been used as workhorses for at least a thousand years. Draft horses have pulled logs out of forests, harvested ice from ponds, and plowed soil around the world. Their strength and stamina made them indispensable in rural areas such as the American Midwest in the 1820s, where they powered such heavy new inventions as the mechanical reaper and thresher. In Europe and the United States, draft horses were often kept by dairies and breweries to haul products in brightly painted advertising wagons. They are still used in some European cities where brewers find horses to be more cost effective than trucks for short hauls. Draft horses and draft-crosses once pulled steam-pumped water trucks and ladder trucks for fire departments. Strength, stamina, and nerves of steel were essential as these horses had to race to fires with their heavy loads. New York City began using fire horses in 1832; by 1906 they had 1500 fire horses in use. As motor vehicles replaced them, many draft breeds came close to extinction. But the efforts of draft horse enthusiasts kept many of the more popular breeds alive, and today there is a resurgence of interest in draft horses for pleasure and work.

Draft horses are popular in show events of all kinds: driving classes, pulling and plowing competitions, jousting tournaments, and vaulting competitions. Vaulting is an equestrian sport in which humans perform freestyle and compulsory movements with an equine partner that is moving in a circle on a lunge line. Vaulting routines consist

Three horses race along a city street to the scene of a fire, pulling a steam-powered water pump and three firemen behind them. Horse-drawn steam engines like this one were used in the great Chicago fire of 1871.

of both gymnastic and dance moves set to music. Vaulting requires a strong, fit horse, and draft horses and draft crosses are frequently used.

In the show ring, some of the more common draft horse show hitches are the team hitch, a pair of horses hitched side by side; a tandem, or two horses, one hitched directly behind the other (this is used when the power of two horses is needed but the path to be negotiated is narrow); three abreast and four abreast, popular farm hitches in which all of the horses are hitched side by side; and four, six, eight, and even sixteen-horse hitches, in which the horses are hitched in sets of twos. There is also a unicorn hitch, a three-horse hitch consisting of two horses hitched together in the back with one horse in front of them as the lead. The unicorn hitch was devised by urban teamsters who needed more power than one pair of horses could provide. Three horses abreast would take up more space than was practical on city streets, so the third horse was hitched in front of the wheelers, or rear horses.

Handling a multiple-horse hitch is a true test of rein-manship and horsemanship. It can be very tricky to keep all the horses under control and pulling their share of the weight. The teamster is judged on how well synchronized the horses are.

Drafts are also used in pulling contests, which showcase their strength. The most successful pulling horses are those who are exercised the most. Like champion weightlifters, pulling horses must be conditioned constantly to keep their muscles and tendons in good shape and to prevent injury. The basic rules of horse pulling are that a team must pull a certain weight over a specified number of feet, usually any-where from 12 to 27 feet. The team has up to three chances to pull the load the required distance. Some pulls are also timed, so the team must not only pull the load the full distance, but pull it within the specified time. Pulling horses are divided into different classes by weight. A team of pulling horses with a combined weight of under 3,200 pounds will be in a different class than a team weighing over 3,200.

What was once done for necessity and to prepare a field for harvest is now done for sport as well. In plow matches horses and their human partners compete to see who can plow the straightest furrow. Draft horses of all breeds are

 Defining Horsepower

The term "horsepower," which is today the commonly accepted unit for measuring power on all types of engines from cars to lawn mowers, first came into use around 1806. It originated with the Scottish inventor and engineer James Watt, who is best known for his improvements to the steam engine. Watt was anxious to demonstrate the efficiency of his new steam engine, and he decided the best way to do this would be to compare the capacity of his machine with that of a horse. In order to compare his machine to a horse, Watt had to quantify the power of a horse, so he had horses lift a weight up from the bottom of a well by pulling horizontally on a rope that passed over a pulley. He determined that, on average, a horse could raise a weight of 100 pounds while walking at a rate of 2.5 miles per hour, or 220 feet per minute. This measurement was calculated as 22,000 foot-pounds (220 feet per minute times a weight of 100 pounds). For reasons that are not clear, Watt raised this amount to 33,000 foot-pounds per minute and established it as the standard unit of horsepower. This remains the unit of power used to rate electric motors, steam engines, and gasoline engines today.

frequent competitors, as are mules. There are classes for walk-behind plows and riding plows. The driver using the walk-behind plow holds up the handles of the plow, which is dragged forward by the horses, causing the plow blade to be dragged into the ground, throwing the dirt up on either side of its path. This process creates a straight furrow, or trough, in the soil in which seeds can be sown. A team of plow horses must work together. The horse on the left walks in the field while the horse on the right walks in the last furrow plowed. The horse walking the furrow must be trained to walk carefully and very straight, so as not to disturb the furrow. Plowing is one of the most tiring tasks a horse can do. It requires tremendous strength to pull a plow down through heavy soil over the course of a day.

Today draft horses work primarily on small farms and logging operations. On the farm they may be put to work harrowing and plowing fields to prepare them for planting, or cutting, raking, and baling hay, which they will eat in winter. Horses are useful on maple sugaring operations because they can drag a sap collection tank into a sugar-bush in winter. Horses can also draw a cultivator between rows of crops to weed and loosen the soil between young plants, reducing the need to use herbicides. Almost any kind of farming equipment can be adapted to horsepower. The major advantage to using horses is that they will go the extra mile when asked, and in addition to their normal strength they can exert tremendous extra reserves of strength for short periods of time—something a tractor can't do. They will also work in mud and snow. Horses have an advantage over other draft animals, too, because, unlike oxen or mules, horses can reproduce. (Oxen are castrated bovines, and mules, the offspring of a horse and a donkey, are usually sterile).

Well into the 20th century, before mechanical fellers, forwarders, and skidders existed, logging was done with horses, oxen, and mules. In the winter, horses would drag heavy sleds laden with logs down hard-packed trails. Today, horse logging persists as a low-impact means of timber harvesting. Horse loggers often work on small woodlots where skid distances are less than a quarter mile, and in areas where machines are forbidden or unable to be driven, such as extremely steep inclines. Unlike machines, horses can skid logs up or down these steep slopes. Landowners who want to harvest timber without the need for creating wide skid roads may choose to use a horse logger instead of a mechanical operator.

While farming and logging are two of the most common uses of draft horses, they aren't the only ones. Draft horses are used to unroll fiberoptic cable up and down steep inclines, harvest commercially valuable seaweed from the ocean, deliver feed to ranch livestock in winter, scour trout spawning beds, and clean up after hurricanes. Draft horses frequently appear in historical re-enactments, and they are commonly used to pull tourist trolleys, hay rides, sleigh rides, and canal boats.

Despite the continued modernization of all aspects of life and work, horses have never gone away. Even after they were no longer essential for transportation or work, horses were kept by those who loved and appreciated them. There are nearly seven million horses in the United States today, used in racing, showing, recreation, and work. Horses are a multi-billion dollar industry, and there are many people whose livelihoods still depend on the horse. Horses in harness have a long history, and their future looks even more promising.

c. **4000** B.C.	Humans first domesticate horses
c. **3000** B.C.	Horses are used to pull war chariots in Mesopotamia
c. **2500** B.C.	Mesopotamian coins depict horses yoked together like oxen
1400 B.C.	The Hittite king Supiluliumas has clay tablets engraved with instructions for selecting, training, and conditioning horses
680 B.C.	Chariot racing makes its Olympic debut
400 B.C.	The Greek horseman Xenophon writes *The Art of Horsemanship*, which advocates the kind treatment of horses
300 B.C.	The breast strap harness is in use in China
1000 A.D.	The invention of the horse collar revolutionizes horsepower
1492	Spanish explorers bring horses to the New World
1631, 1632	Gustavus Adolphus of Sweden uses horses to mobilize his army's artillery and win decisive victories at the battles of Breitenfeld and Lutzen
1706	The first stagecoach service begins operating in England
1750	Improvements to British roads make carriage driving popular
1784	Horse-drawn mail delivery coaches begin regular service in England
1832	The New York City Fire Department begins using horses
1910	1,750,000 horse-drawn vehicles are made in the United States; 80,000 automobiles are also manufactured
1940	The USTA is formed; pari-mutuel harness racing begins
1946	The mobile starting gate is introduced to harness racing
1968	Combined Driving becomes an organized sport
1980	Niatross becomes the first Standardbred to break 1:50
2001	The horse population in the United States reaches seven million

GLOSSARY

Artillery—large crew-served mounted weapons such as cannons

Blinders—two flaps on a horse's bridle designed to prevent sight of objects behind or to the side

Breast-strap harness—a light driving harness in which the strain of the load is born by the horse's breast

Breeching—the part of a harness that goes behind a horse's rump and serves to help the horse back up and brake the load

Chariot—a two-wheeled horse-drawn vehicle of ancient times used in processions, races, and battle

Collar—part of a draft horse harness that goes around the neck and rests on the shoulders, where it takes the strain when a load is drawn

Destrier—name for a war horse and a charger used in tournaments

Hobbles—item worn by pacers to prevent them from breaking stride

Pacer—a horse whose predominant gait is a pace, in which both legs on one side of the body move forward at the same time

Phaeton—a light four-wheeled horse-drawn vehicle

Shadow roll—a puffy roll attached to the noseband of a horse's bridle to prevent it from seeing directly below; often used in harness and Thoroughbred racing

Shafts—the poles of a cart between which a single horse is hitched to a vehicle

Singletree—the bar to which the traces of a harness are fastened and by which a vehicle or implement is drawn; also called a whiffletree

Stagecoach—a horse-drawn passenger and mail coach running on a regular schedule between stops

Sulky—a lightweight cart used in Standardbred racing

Travois—a wheel-less horse-drawn vehicle used by Plains Indians

Trotter—a horse whose predominant gait is the trot, in which the opposite hind and forelegs move forward at the same time

Wheeler—name for a horse placed in the back of a hitch, closest to the wheels

Yoke—a wooden frame joining two draft animals, such as oxen, at the neck in order for them to work together

Bean, Heike and Sarah Blanchard. *Carriage Driving: A Logical Approach Through Dressage Training.* New York: Howell Books, 1992.

Ganton, Doris L. *Breaking and Training the Driving Horse: A Detailed and Comprehensive Study.* North Hollywood, California: Wilshire Book Company, 1985.

Miller, Lynn R. *The Work Horse Handbook.* Sisters, Oregon: Small Farmer's Journal, Inc., 1998.

Peterson, Chris, and Alvis Upitis. *Horsepower.* Honesdale, Pennsylvania: Boyds Mill Press, 1997.

Telleen, Maurice. *The Draft Horse Primer.* Waverly, Iowa: The Draft Horse Journal, Inc., 1993.

Twelveponies, Mary. *Starting the Colt: First Lessons in Riding and Driving.* Boston: Houghton Mifflin Co., 1992.

Walrond, Sallie. *Handling Your Problem Horse: Causes, Preventions, and Cures of Over 50 Problems Associated with Riding, Driving, and Handling.* Stillwater, Minnesota: Voyageur Press, 1999.

Websites

www.ustrotting.com
The official website of the United States Trotting Association offers harness racing news, race results, and information on Standardbred horses

www.uset.org
The official website of the United States Equestrian Team has links to the sport of combined driving

www.americandrivingsociety.org
The American Driving Society website offers information on driving competitions as well as links to other driving websites

www.drafthorsejournal.com
The online version of the Draft Horse Journal has information on draft horses and mules, links to other draft horse sites, and interactive bulletin boards

www.imh.org
The International Museum of the Horse, one of the largest online museums in the world, hosts interactive exhibits on the history of the horse as well as information on horse breeds of the world

page:

MARY E. HULL is the author of several books for young adults, including *Censorship in America: A Reference Handbook* (ABC-CLIO 1999) and *Struggle and Love* (Chelsea House 1997), which was selected by the New York Public Library Association as a "Best Book for the Teen Age." A 1995 graduate of Brown University, Ms. Hull works as a book packager and has produced numerous books for young readers, including Chelsea House's *Composite Guide*, *Figure Skating Legends*, *Pro Wrestling Legends*, and *Horse Library* series. In her spare time she enjoys driving and riding her Belgian draft horse.